ADHD

Stories Of Those With Attention Deficit Hyperactivity Disorder And How They Overcame It

By

Grant Anderson

Table of Contents

Introduction

First off, I'd like to thank you for purchasing "ADHD: Stories Of Those With Attention Deficit Hyperactivity Disorder And How They Overcame It". By purchasing this book either you or someone you love is suffering from ADHD. Purchasing this book was an excellent first step to gain some information on this important topic, as ADHD is something that millions of people are suffering from worldwide. I've had close family members struggle with their ADHD. The good news is you can find ways to overcome this disorder with hard work and treatment.

My older sister has suffered from ADHD all my life. Back when we were young, illnesses like this often did not get diagnosed so we just thought she was being difficult and liked the attention she got from acting out. My sister wasn't diagnosed until later in life when her son started having difficulty in school and was diagnosed with ADHD. It was at this point she realized she had been suffering from many of the same symptoms since she was a little girl, got diagnosed herself, and started seeking treatment.

Over the next few years, both my sister and my nephew learned different methods to help them deal with their ADHD, where it didn't negatively affect their day-to-day lives. They still struggle at times, but they are able to go on and accomplish what they set out to without too much disturbance.

* * *

So, what is ADHD? Well, ADHD or Attention Deficit Hyperactivity Disorder is the most common mental disorder diagnosed in children, and can carry into adulthood. People suffering from ADHD are often unable to control all of their impulses and can become overly hyperactive at times. People suffering from this disorder will often have difficulty paying attention for any extended period of time, affecting schoolwork, jobs, and personal relationships.

ADHD is more prevalent in boys than it is in girls. Normally, this disorder gets diagnosed during a child's schooling, when they begin having difficultly staying focused and performing their schoolwork properly.

Adults diagnosed with ADHD often have trouble being organized, managing time, holding down jobs, and setting goals. Their personal relationships will normally suffer, and they will often develop self-esteem issues and addiction issues.

There are different severity levels when dealing with ADHD and therefore different types of treatments and medications are used to treat them. I'll discuss all of these in further detail throughout the book. I'll also go over some of the symptoms and main causes or risk factors linked to ADHD, and what actions you should take if you think someone you love needs to be treated.

Many people suffering from ADHD are able to live happy, successful, full lives once treated. It's important to always continue monitoring the symptoms and visit the doctor on a regular basis. Occasionally treatments and medications that once worked will stop being effective. Many people will have to alter their treatment plan at least once in their lifetime. For many, ADHD symptoms begin to lessen in adulthood, and some people are even able to eventually forego treatment altogether

This book will go over ADHD in depth and will also share with you a bunch of stories of people like my sister and nephew who've lived with their disorder and have learned ways to overcome it. I'll go over the different ways they dealt with their issues and took back control of their lives. I truly hope their experiences, and how they persevered, will help to inspire you or your loved ones to one day do the same.

Let's get started!

CHAPTER ONE

An Introduction To ADHD

In this chapter, you will learn:

- An Introduction to ADHD

- How Does ADHD Get Diagnosed

- My Sister's Life With ADHD

- How to Help A Friend or Loved One With ADHD

- How to Help Yourself If You Think You Have ADHD

An Introduction to ADHD

Throughout the course of this book I will present stories of people who suffer from ADHD, and I'll share with you how they were able to fight through adversity and emerge from the other side a much happier and better functioning person. Each of these stories will capture a main factor common to ADHD and show what methods they used to overcome their own set of issues.

First, however, I'd like to share a little more about ADHD, the different types of ADHD, what its main causes and risk factors are, and some of the symptoms it can cause in those affected.

ADHD is one of the most common mental disorders world-wide. No one reason for ADHD has ever been found. Most experts believe it's brought on by a variety of different factors. ADHD is normally separated into three different types, which I'll go over in the next section. ADHD isn't preventable or curable. However, treatment, education, and medication, can help someone with ADHD successfully manage all of their symptoms.

The 3 main types of ADHD include:

1. Predominantly Inattentive Type – Someone who suffers from this form of ADHD will show more symptoms of inattention rather than hyperactivity and impulsiveness. People with this type of ADHD can also have issues with impulse control and hyperactivity, but those factors aren't considered to be the main characteristics that they present. This form of ADHD has been found to be more prevalent in girls than it is in boys.

People who suffer from predominantly inattention ADHD often:

7

Get bored very quickly.

Get distracted very easily.

Miss a lot of the details.

Don't seem to be listening at times.

Lose items needed in the completion of tasks. (e.g. paper & pens for schoolwork).

Have trouble staying focused on a singular task.

Have trouble keeping their thoughts properly organized.

Have trouble learning new ideas and information.

Move at a slower pace and often appear to be daydreaming.

Have difficulty following even simple directions.

Have trouble processing information quickly and accurately.

2. Predominantly Hyperactive-Impulsive Type – This kind of ADHD is often characterized by hyperactivity and impulsiveness. People can still display some signs of inattention but it's not as noticeable as the other symptoms. Children suffering from this type of ADHD are often a disruption to other children around them, and can make learning more difficult not only for themselves, but also for the people they're disrupting.

People who suffer from predominantly hyperactive-impulsive ADHD often:

Have trouble sitting still.

Talk constantly.

Feel restless and have issues with fidgeting and squirming.

Playing with / or touching objects, even if it is inappropriate to your task on hand.

Difficultly with activities that are quiet in nature.

Feeling impatient.

Not thinking about consequences before acting.

Making inappropriate comments, or constantly interrupting people.

3. *Combination Type* – People who have this type of ADHD have a relatively equal mixture of both the above types. Generally, they have at least six symptoms of both hyperactivity/impulsive and inattention. As per The National Institute of Mental Health, most children with ADHD are diagnosed as having a combination type.

As you can see just from the list of types of ADHD above, this is a neurobehavioral disorder that can severely impact the lives of those suffering from it. Being held back by your ADHD is no way to properly live a productive and meaningful life. It took my sister a few years to really get her symptoms under control. It was a real struggle at times for her to find the motivation and strength to fight back and overcome all of her issues. No matter what type of ADHD you or a loved one is dealing with, there is help out there for you. All you have to do is reach out to someone and take it.

Some of the primary causes and risk factors include:

Heredity – ADHD is often found in families. In my family, both my sister and nephew suffer from ADHD.

Brain Changes – Children suffering from ADHD often have less activity in the section of the brain that is responsible for controlling attention span.

Chemical Imbalance – People with ADHD often have brain chemicals that are out of balance.

Poor Nutrition – Not having a proper diet can affect brain development and causes imbalances.

Bad Lifestyle Choices – Substance abuse, drinking and smoking during a pregnancy can affect a baby's developing brain, leading to changes and imbalances that can result in ADHD.

Toxins – Being exposed to things like lead can negatively affect brain development in children.

Brain Disorder and Injury – Damaging the front of your brain, known as the frontal lobe, will lead to problems processing emotions and controlling impulses.

ADHD is not caused by sugar, food allergies, poor schooling, or watching too much television. These things are often incorrectly associated with ADHD. I hear these things being thrown around all the time by people not educated in this disorder and I just wanted to clarify that for those of you that may have heard similar things.

ADHD cannot be cured. But if you spot it early and have a good plan for treatment in place, you can effectively manage your symptoms. The symptoms of your ADHD will often help to determine the proper course of treatment. Understanding what the underlying symptoms behind your ADHD are, can help to determine what types of treatments will be most effective at managing your issues.

I broke down the different types of ADHD above and what some of the symptoms were for each. However, the symptoms seen in children and adults can also differ. So, i'll break down the symptoms commonly seen in children and adults separately.

Some of the main ADHD symptoms in children include:

Gets easily distracted.

Never appears to listen.

Can't finish things or follow directions.

Forgets their daily plans or responsibilities.

Makes lots of mistakes and can't pay attention.

Can't stay organized.

Can't sit still for long.

Will lose things often.

Constantly daydreams.

Fidgets, bounces, and squirms when sitting.

Can't play quietly for long.

Always wants to be moving. Is always on the "go".

Excessive talking.

Has difficulty waiting their turn.

Blurts answers out and interrupts others often.

Some of the main ADHD symptoms in adults include:

Anxiety.

Trouble controlling their anger.

Forgetfulness and chronic lateness.

Problems functioning at work.

Low self-esteem.

Impulsiveness.

Addiction or substance abuse.

Procrastination.

Unorganized.

Easily frustrated.

Difficulty concentrating (e.g. trouble reading).

Chronic boredom.

Relationship problems.

Depression.

Mood swings.

People that suffer from ADHD won't all have the exact same symptoms. The duration, severity, and frequency of symptoms will depend on each individual. I know that in my sister's case, although she suffered from many of these issues, she never had any addiction issues or anger issues.

Some of these symptoms are simpler to overcome than others. Often my sister still experiences a few of these symptoms. However, now she has the tools to deal with her ADHD and she finds that she's able to work through most of her symptoms without letting them negatively impact her life.

How Does ADHD Get Diagnosed

So you're not sure if you or a loved one has ADHD but you know there's a bigger problem going on. Maybe they have a few of the symptoms above and want to know if ADHD is the root cause of these issues.

My advice is to go and visit your doctor. There is no one test that can determine if you have ADHD. ADHD is only diagnosed after someone has shown all or some of the ADHD symptoms listed above on a continual basis for a period of six months or longer. Also, these symptoms need to be in more than just a single setting. A person's specific set of symptoms will classify what type of ADHD they're suffering from.

In children, normally a health care provider – like a psychiatrist or pediatrician – can diagnose a case of ADHD using the standard guidelines put forth by the American Psychiatric Association's Diagnostic and Statistical Manual. Coming to a proper diagnosis involves gathering information on the child from caregivers, schools, and parents. They will also take into account how the child's behavior compares to other children of similar age.

To get a proper ADHD diagnosis, the child should get a full physical examination; this includes hearing and vision screenings. Also, the use of Neuropsychiatric EEG Assessment Aid, or (NEBA) has been approved by the FDA as a noninvasive way to scan beta and theta wave levels. It has been shown that children with ADHD have a higher theta/beta ratio than kids without it. This test has been approved for children between 6 and 17 years old. It is only meant as one part of a complete psychological and medical exam.

A complete medical history should also be conducted by the health care provider, to screen for other things that may affect the child's behavior. There are certain conditions which present like ADHD but upon closer examination, are in fact caused by other issues.

These other issues are:

Undetected seizures.

Major life changes (death, recent move, divorce).

13

Sleep problems.

Thyroid problems.

Lead toxicity.

Depression.

Anxiety.

Oftentimes, parents who think their children might have ADHD end up learning that one of the issues listed above is actually the real cause behind their child's issues. Getting a proper diagnosis is incredibly important to getting your child the correct treatment plan.

In adults, diagnosing ADHD is not as easy as it is for children. Like in my sister's case, she only recognized the ADHD symptoms in herself once her son was diagnosed. In some people, they end up learning about their condition only after they've sought treatment for anxiety, depression, or other ADHD symptoms they were experiencing.

In addition, as I mentioned above, adults have additional symptoms besides the one's normally found in children. If these symptoms can't be managed, they can lead to social, emotional, financial, and occupational problems.

Adults with ADHD need to have current and persistent symptoms that date back to childhood. ADHD symptoms can continue on as problems long into adulthood for around half of all children with ADHD.

To get an accurate ADHD diagnosis as an adult you'll need:

Psychological testing.

A thorough history of the adult's behavior when they were a child.

An interview with either a parent, close friend, or life partner.

A physical exam, including neurological testing.

Once all those tests have been completed, the health care provider will be able to come up with a proper diagnosis and determine a path of treatment if necessary.

My Sister's Life With ADHD

My sister Ellen always felt different from other people but didn't know why. From the time she was a little girl, she had a problem sitting still and keeping track of things. She used to get in trouble all the time during school for daydreaming and not paying attention. Her schoolwork always suffered, and she found sitting through a day of class to be the height of boredom.

Back when my sister was younger, no one was really aware of ADHD, so her behavior was written off as Ellen being difficult or a bit flighty and ditsy. Ellen always thought the way she was feeling was the way everyone felt, so she ignored her symptoms and continued to struggle all the way into adulthood.

Ellen eventually got married and had my nephew Jack. Everything continued on for a few years until Jack started school and his teachers contacted her about Jack's issues during school. As far as Ellen had known he was fine, so at first she was a little resistant to the idea that something could be wrong. It was only when Jack's teacher told her what she thought the issue was, that Ellen did some research and realized there might be a problem not only with Jack but herself too.

Jack saw all the doctors and had all the tests needed to diagnose ADHD, and sure enough, he was diagnosed with the combination type. Once he was diagnosed and given an initial plan for treatment, Ellen realized she had dealt with most of the same issues for all of her life. She decided to get evaluated as well, and was eventually diagnosed with ADHD.

It's been a few years now, and both Jack and my sister have responded incredibly well to the treatment and medications they're on. Ellen still can't believe she went so long feeling the way she used to. She no longer feels out of control, and is enjoying a new sense of inner peace that she's only now been able to find in her life. Not only has her outlook improved, but she also got a new and better job, and she's made a lot of great new friends during the treatment process.

As for Jack, he's doing much better in school and is able to be a normal kid again. It took some time for him to learn to slow down and focus, but he's made huge strides from where he started out.

I want to stress that they didn't get better immediately. It took some time for treatment to work, and to get the medications right. During the course of this book, I'll touch on various different methods to help you deal with ADHD. I urge you to try each of these and see which ones make are the most effective in your life.

While my sister and nephew's case isn't nearly as extreme as many of the other people I've met over the years since, it did hold them back from doing a lot of things, especially in my sister's case.

Now they both lead happier and more productive lives. Sometimes their symptoms do act up, and on once occasion my sister did have to switch up her medication. However, in general, they've learned ways to overcome their ADHD and that means it's possible that you can to.

How to Help A Friend or Loved One With ADHD

Many families and well-meaning friends often make mistakes when trying to support someone they care about suffering from ADHD, mainly because they don't properly understand the disorder. For instance, many people often think ADHD is some type of academic problem, or that it's solely an issue of not being able to focus.

In reality, ADHD is a disorder related to our executive functioning. This functioning involves the numerous cognitive processes we use in order to enable us to move towards our goals. It helps us to do things like decision making, prioritizing, and organizing our time properly.

It is quite common to see loved ones dismissing the intelligence of a person with ADHD when that person can't do something as simple as keeping a home properly organized. Worse still, it undermines the struggles of the person dealing with ADHD. One of example of this is saying to the person, "Anyone can organize a desk. It's not difficult, even a little kid can do it". However, it's not that a person with ADHD doesn't know how to do a task; instead, it's that they can't effectively involve their executive functioning to do the tasks required to get it done.

Once you begin to understand that sufferers of ADHD have an issue with their executive functioning, you begin to realize it can dramatically affect every facet of their life.

Here are some simple ways you can help a family member or loved one:

1. Get educated – This is probably the most powerful and meaningful form of support. Join a support group, read some books on ADHD, really get to know the disorder.

2. Ask – It's a simple yet powerful thing. Ask your loved one what they might need. Just lend a hand where possible and try to be an empathetic person they can turn to. For adults with ADHD, it's incredibly helpful to have a person they can vent their issues and frustrations to.

3. Point out your loved one strengths – Many people suffering from ADHD also suffer from bouts of low self-esteem. Giving positive reinforcement will go a long way towards helping them.

4. Offer to stay with them when doing a task – If a person with ADHD is having a difficult time with a certain task, offer your time and stay with them as they work on what they need to get done. This kind of support can go a long way.

5. Avoid judgment – You'll find that people with ADHD are very sensitive to getting judged by others. Try not to use words like strange, weird, crazy, or odd when around them. Many people with ADHD who hear those words begin to feel inferior to the people around them. Also, try and avoid offering what is known as "toxic help". This is when you offer to help a loved one, and lend a hand, but in the process you demoralize them. For example, you offer to help clean their house while emphasizing that it's a total disaster area.

Amy & Tina's Story

Amy and Tina had been best friends since they were little girls. Amy was always bouncing off the walls and Tina was a bit more bookish and laid back. Once they reached the 5th grade, Amy began showing more and more symptoms of ADHD. Tina knew something was off with her friend because she was constantly bouncing off the walls and would forget things they were supposed to do after school together. Tina told her mom about how Amy was acting, who in turn spoke with Amy's parents after noticing a lot of the same things in her dealings when Amy stayed at their place.

At first, Amy's parents thought it was just normal growing pains and chalked it up to the fact that people go through different phases. It was only when she came home with her next report card and saw that Amy had failed two subjects she was normally good at, that her parents became concerned. Amy's parents reached out to her teachers who said that they had noticed also noticed a change in Amy's behavior. It wasn't long after that, that Amy was officially diagnosed with combination type ADHD and began treatment.

Tina's parents explained Amy's situation to her and Tina, being the good friend she was, learnt a bit more about ADHD on her own. Tina made it a point not to treat her friend differently and it really meant a lot to Amy. Today, the two are both in high school, they're still best friends, and they haven't let ADHD get in the way of enjoying their lives.

How to Help Yourself If You Have ADHD

If you have some of the ADHD symptoms I discussed above, here are some things you can try and do to help yourself. People with ADHD often find it incredibly difficult to seek help, stay focused, or take action. Just know that you can do it and once you do, things will gradually start to get better.

Don't wait too long before getting evaluated and treated. Chances are that if it's still bothering you now and you're in adulthood, these symptoms have persisted for a long while now. Seeing a doctor and getting treatment recommendations may be a great option to take. Most people respond well to their ADHD medications. However, there are some alternative lifestyle changes you can make in order to lessen your symptoms. It may not eliminate them altogether, but it will help you feel much more in control of yourself.

Don't stop learning about your disorder too – the more information you have and the more strategies you learn, the better you'll be able to determine the treatments that work best for you. Everyone responds differently, so some people will have more or less success following certain treatment plans than others.

Try and focus on social skills training. The more you work on these skills, the more you'll begin to notice when your symptoms are taking a turn for the worse, and the quicker you'll be able to reverse course and get them back under control.

Try and make plans to help you stay organized better. Also limit your distractions by turning off music or TV while working on a task, and using noise canceling headphones in a louder environment when you need to keep focused. A great tool that has helped me stay focused on the bigger picture and keep on task is an all-in-one spreadsheet package found on GoalSettingChallenge.com (see BONUS #2). It's amazing what a good goal tracker does for your motivation and this one is especially effective, as you are able to compete against your friends using a live updated leaderboard while also comparing your stats with each other.

No matter how you're feeling, also try and exercise and stay active. Even if you're just going to a movie, get out of the house and do something. Spend time with friends and confide in people you're close to. The more you face your problems head on, the better prepared you'll be to overcome them.

Don't expect your ADHD symptoms to go away overnight. This is a process. It will take some time, but with proper treatment you can begin to get better.

By following the above steps you'll be putting yourself in the best position to succeed. The more you work at getting better, the easier it will become. Soon the things above will become second nature and will no longer feel like work at all.

Danny's Story

Danny was diagnosed with ADHD when he was little. His symptoms continued into adulthood unchecked. Up until this point in his life, Danny had refused to stick with his treatments and medication. He always thought he didn't need any help, knowing that he could do it himself if he really tried.

It wasn't until Danny got a girl he been dating pregnant that he started to really take his issues seriously. For years he had bounced around from job to job, never staying anywhere for too long at once. He never went to college, so he mostly stuck to menial jobs doing labor-intensive work.

However, now that he was going to be a dad, Danny realized that the way he was living his life wasn't going to cut it if he wanted to raise and support a family. Danny knew that his ADHD was holding him back, so he finally started getting treatment. He began seeing a therapist, exercising regularly, and even started taking night classes to try and get a degree.

Danny knew he wasn't going to get better overnight, but maybe by the time the baby came, he would be in a place where he could not only better financially support his new family, but also deal with the stress and responsibilities that come with raising a child.

It's been a few years since Danny started to try and make a change. He began working as a licensed cooling and heating tech last fall, and has noticed a major difference in his ability to focus and keep a clear head. He no longer feels overwhelmed and is enjoying life with his baby daughter.

CHAPTER TWO

ADHD Treatments & Medications

In this chapter, you will learn:

- A Guide to ADHD Treatments

- A Guide to ADHD Medications

A Guide to ADHD Treatments

In this section, I'm going to touch on a few of the different ADHD treatments available. For each treatment type, I'll also share the story of someone I know, relating how they've used those treatments to help improve their lives.

Just as the causes and symptoms of ADHD differ from one another, so are the methods of treatment. What works for some won't work for others. There is no one magic treatment that will work for everyone. You should take the time to really explore each of the treatment options I'll present to you below, and find the treatments that work best for you.

Treatment for ADHD has two major components — 1) psychotherapy interventions and 2) medications. There has been an enormous amount of excellent research that shows that using medication by itself won't address a lot of the core issues someone with ADHD deals with. Medication will give some immediate relief, but it's by using them in concert with the different treatments I'll be discussing in this section, that sufferers find the most amount of long-term benefit. People living with ADHD need to learn the different skills necessary to live with the disorder successfully.

1. Psychotherapy

There has been a few decades worth of research now that shows the effectiveness of different psychotherapies in relation to treating ADHD, both in adults and children. Whether you want to just go with psychotherapy or use it along with medication, both methods are clinically accepted.

The most common form of psychotherapy in treating ADHD is referred to as cognitive behavioral therapy or CBT. CBT is one of the most widely used psychological treatments as it is based on the latest scientific research, and therefore it is usually highly effective. Often therapists will use either cognitive therapy or behavioral therapy, depending on what they think is best for the patient.

Cognitive therapies are more focused on the mind. The person suffering from ADHD first talks about their upsetting feelings and thoughts, while the therapist explores any self-defeating thinking patterns. Through this, the patient also learns new and alternative methods for handling their emotions, raising their self-esteem, coping with daily problems, controlling their aggression, focusing, and improving their attention span.

This type of therapy can also be good for helping families deal with disruptive behavior by developing techniques for improving their kids' behaviors. It will also teach a person with ADHD improved self-awareness and compassion.

On the other hand, behavioral therapy is a specific kind of psychotherapy that is focused on ways to handle and deal with more immediate issues. It digs into dealing with coping behaviors and thinking patterns directly, without the need to try and understand the pattern's origins. The aim of this therapy is behavior change, like organizing schoolwork or tasks in a better manner, or handling emotionally charged situations as they occur. In this therapy, a child might be told to monitor their own actions and then treat themselves to rewards for any positive behavior, like thinking through a situation instead of just reacting to it.

Kevin's Story

Kevin struggled for all of his adolescent life. School was incredibly boring but he naturally picked things up quickly so he was able to make it through without having to ever pay too much attention or focus to hard on studying. Kevin's issues continued on into high school and increasingly started affecting his social interactions. Kevin knew something wasn't right because none of his friends were experiencing the same issues as him.

Kevin knew he needed help. More help than he was able to provide himself. And although ADHD and mental disorders weren't a topic of conversation in his family, he knew that he needed to make a big change in his life or else he would always feel out of control. Kevin started seeing someone that a friend recommended and was diagnosed with ADHD.

For Kevin, getting that diagnosis was difficult. There is so much negativity around the issue of mental disorders, that it made him feel inferior to everyone around him. Luckily, he knew he needed to see someone, and once he started therapy, his therapist was able to help Kevin overcome the self-esteem issues he was dealing with, and understand that there was nothing he should feel ashamed about. He had a medical disorder that needed treatment. It was as simple as that.

After working with his therapist and starting a cognitive behavioral therapy program based around confronting and challenging his past, Kevin began to slowly get better. Kevin soon began to realize and understand that his issues were issues that he could handle and overcome as long as he was willing to put in the work and continual effort.

Nowadays, Kevin still struggles with ADHD, and still attends therapy every week to help keep himself on the right path. However, he no longer lets his symptoms rule his life. Kevin is set to attend community college next year and wants to work in the mental health field giving back to the community that embraced him and gave him a greater purpose in life

2. Social Skills Training

This important training is mostly for children with ADHD and teaches the behavior necessary to maintain and develop strong social relationships. It also teaches how to improve social skills with an emphasis on things like sharing, how to respond to teasing, waiting until it's your turn, and asking for help when it's needed.

Most kids learn these skills naturally – they are not normally taught by parents or in a classroom, but are usually learned through watching and repeating the behaviors of other people around them. However, children suffering from ADHD have a more difficult time learning these crucial skills and knowing how to implement them into their daily lives.

Having a therapy session for social skills training allows the person to learn and use the skills they've learned in a nurturing environment. It gives the person a safe place where they can practice without fear of being made fun of or looked down upon.

Some of the skills taught include the art of having conversations with those around you, learning to see things from another person's perspective, asking questions, listening, the importance of making eye contact, and how to read and interpret gestures and body language.

These training sessions are normally done in the therapists office, with either just the therapist or with the parents and therapist. Once the parents learn how to teach the skills, they can begin doing so at home for further reinforcement. The therapist will also teach a person what behaviors are appropriate in which situations. They will go over facial cues and different tones of voice.

Rosie's Story

Rosie always had trouble making friends and dealing with kids in school. People often got fed up with her enormous amount of energy, her inability to sit still, and her knack for constantly interrupting people and blurting out whatever was going on in her head.

One of her teachers recognized all that she had all of the symptoms of ADHD, and Rosie was eventually diagnosed. However, even as her symptoms began to lessen and get under control, Rosie was still having difficulty relating to other people and making new friends.

Eventually her therapist suggested social skills training to her parents as a way to help solve some of these lingering issues. Rosie began learning how to properly interact with other children, how to read body language, and how to interpret facial cues.

This training went on at both the office and at home with her parents over the course of many months. Progress was slow at first, but gradually Rosie began getting the hang of it. Eventually she was able to put her skills into use in real life and finally started to make new friends and interact with her peers without feeling left out or disconnected.

Now Rosie has a good social life – she plays soccer with friends and has really put the skills she learned to good use. Rosie still has some difficulties with her schoolwork, but her parents are confident that in time she'll improve in that area.

3. Support Groups

Mutual support groups are extremely beneficial for both the parents and the individuals suffering from ADHD. Having a sense of regularly connecting with other people living with the same type of issues can lead to problem sharing, openness, and a willingness to give and receive advice.

This is a great environment for sharing fears, concerns, and other things that are irritating or frustrating, all whilst being in the confines of a compassionate and caring environment. Here, people are able to vent and let off some steam, knowing that they're not alone in their illness.

These groups can also present wonderful learning opportunities. My sister's group often invites guest lecturers and experts in the field to come discuss topics and field questions. Another positive of support groups is that they allow people to network and share helpful resources. For example, getting a referral to a good specialist in the field through one of the members in the group.

Sally's Story

Sally grew up in foster care. She bounced around in the system until she was 18 and then went out on her own. She was never diagnosed as a child with ADHD. It wasn't until she was struggling to survive on her own that she went to a doctor to help her with concentration problems. She had terrible bouts of forgetfulness and it had already cost her a job she had thoroughly enjoyed. She was determined not to let that happen again.

Her doctor took her history and sent her for further evaluation, where she was eventually diagnosed with ADHD. Sally didn't have a family or any type of real support system, so she took her doctor's advice, and started attending a support group in addition to her therapy treatments.

Sally really noticed a difference once she was able to connect with other people and share her story. This type of environment really helped her maintain the proper attitude and mindset needed when trying to deal with her set of issues.

Her bouts of forgetfulness happen much less frequently now, and her overall well-being has improved dramatically over the past year or so. She attributes much of this to the friendships she has made in her support group, and the ability to be herself without feeling like something was wrong with her. It really gave her the strength and confidence to stick to her treatment plan and work towards getting better.

4. Special Education Classes

Many kids suffer academic difficulties due to their ADHD. Most parents don't realize that public schools are required by law to provide special educational services to those children who are in need of it.

Special education classes can be a great place for kids with ADHD to get the structure and attention they need and which they wouldn't otherwise get in a normal classroom environment. Parents may need to jump through a few hoops in order to get their child placed in one of these classes, but it offers a lot of accommodations that are specifically designed to meet your kid's educational needs.

Some of the things included are:

Allowing extra time during testing.

Reducing the amount of homework assignments.

Providing certain assistance with organizational and planning skills.

Simplifying any instructions given about assignments.

Allowing the use of a tape recorder.

Using some behavioral modification techniques during class.

Having computer aided instructions.

If your child is suffering from ADHD and it's affecting their schoolwork, look into getting them placed in a special education class that can help them from getting left behind academically.

Tara's Story

Tara was diagnosed with ADHD in the third grade. She began social skills training and other therapy treatments but even after another year or so, she was still struggling academically. While her social life had improved and she was able to sit through class, her grades had only gotten worse since she had started treatment.

It was at this point that Tara's parents were clued in about their rights to have Tara placed in a special education class that could tailor a plan around the type of help she needed. It took some time for Tara to get placed in a class but once she did, her parents noticed a big difference in her grades.

Tara was a smart girl but the normal classroom environment just wasn't set up to deal with what she needed in order to be a successful student. Once she got into a class where she got the specific help she required, things began to turn around for her. Now Tara is in the 6th grade and has been performing better than ever before. This has improved not only her grades, but it has also raised her self-esteem and given her a new sense of confidence that she didn't have previously.

A Guide to ADHD Medications

In past years, most ADHD treatments were centered on taking medication. Most commonly, ADHD sufferers were prescribed stimulant medications like Adderall or Ritalin. These types of medications are fast acting, well tolerated and usually have fewer side effects. These medications also have extensive research backing their effectiveness in treating ADHD.

Children can vary in how they respond to medication. Finding a combination with the most efficacy and the fewest side effects can be challenging. Your child's physician will try to discover the dose and type of medication that will work best for your child. Many times, a doctor will have you switch medications if one isn't appearing to be effective enough after trying it for a few weeks.

Some of the side effects that occur from taking stimulant medications include headaches, reduced appetite, irritability, feeling jittery, depression, anxiety, increased blood pressure, sleeping problems, paranoia, and gastrointestinal issues. If you begin to present any of these symptoms while on medication, consult your doctor and determine the best course of action.

Many parents are concerned about the safety of stimulant medications. However, these medications aren't addictive and they don't produce any type of "high" in a person with ADHD who is taking them. Why they don't overstimulate people with ADHD is still unknown by researchers. However, they do know that these medications work for most ADHD patients who take them, and are among the most effective ways to treat someone's ADHD symptoms.

ADHD Medications

Some of the main stimulant medications prescribed today include methylphenidate (Ritalin, Metadate, Concerta, Methylin) and amphetamines (Dexedrine, Adderall, and Dextrostat).

Although it might seem risky to be taking stimulants, research shows that when taken as directed by your doctor, these are an effective and safe treatment for ADHD.

ADHD drug treatments have been going on for decades now. Some of the very best results are found using the drugs I've listed down below. The list includes the name of the drug with the minimum approved age for taking it.

Common drugs and approved age for each

Adderall – 3 years and older.

Concerta – 6 years and older.

Daytrana – 6 years and older.

Dexedrine – 3 years and older.

Dextrostat – 3 years and older.

Focalin – 6 years and older.

Metadate – 6 years and older.

Ritalin – 6 years and older.

Strattera – 6 years and older.

Tenex - 12 years and older.

Vyvanse – 6 years and older.

These drugs are often very beneficial in curbing both impulsiveness and hyperactivity. They can help an individual focus better, work more efficiently, and learn easier. These drugs can also help with coordination issues.

While under medical supervision of a doctor, these drugs are all quite safe and won't make the children "high", although they might begin to feel a little different than normal. Research has shown that substance abuse rates are actually lower in those teenagers that have ADHD and are on medication than those who stopped taking their medication.

Most stimulant drugs come in either long-term or short-term forms, and some may come as sustained release – these are taken each morning and remain effective all day long. Your physician will prescribe the form that will be most suitable for your specific situation.

About 10% of all children will see no benefit from using stimulant medications, even after changing brands or adjusting dosage levels. In those cases, a doctor may prescribe antidepressants either alone or to take in tandem with your stimulant medications.

Some newer non-stimulant medications, like Strattera and Vyvanse, can offer benefits that are similar to how stimulants work, but act differently on the brain. Some people who have issues with stimulants may find they tolerate these forms of medications better.

Using medication is often considered to be most helpful if used in addition to some form of therapy or self-help treatment. Medication is good for taking the edge off, but as I mentioned above, dealing with the root cause of your disorder is the best method for dealing with your ADHD in the long run.

How should you take your medication?

Any medications need to be taken regularly for them to be effective. You need to continue taking your medication, even once you're feeling better, in order to help prevent your ADHD symptoms from coming back.

You should only ever stop taking your medication under your doctor's strict supervision. Many medications need to be stopped gradually in order to give your body proper time to adjust.

Also, if you find that one particular type of medication isn't working, you should really consider switching to a different medication. Studies have shown that people who did not show any improvements after being on one form of medication had a higher chance of overcoming their ADHD symptoms once they began a new form of medication, or added another medication to the current one they were already taking.

When taking medications, if you start having any unusual or weird side effects, you need to immediately contact your doctor. Also, I advise you closely monitor your symptoms when you first start a new medication. Keep a log of your symptoms and whether they're improving or getting worse. The more information you have, the better you and your doctor can fine-tune your medication dosage to get the optimal effect.

Jessa's Story

Jessa was always a hyperactive little girl. She didn't know the meaning of the term 'sit still'. From the moment she woke up until the moment she passed out at night, Jessa was running to and fro causing all sorts of trouble.

At first, Jessa's mom simply ignored the signs. However, a year later, Jessa began acting out in school, getting into trouble for being a disturbance, and just being difficult to deal with in general.

Jessa's mom took her to their family doctor and Jessa was eventually diagnosed with ADHD. The news actually came with a little bit of relief for her mom, because now she knew what steps she needed to take in order to help her little girl.

Jessa started therapy and her mom gave her social skills training every day after school. At first, Jessa's mom was resistant to the idea of medicating her daughter. The idea of giving a child stimulants seemed like an unwise decision to make. Unfortunately, however, therapy didn't help curb Jessa's symptoms as much as she had hoped. She was still having a lot of difficulty focusing, doing her homework and keeping still for any period of time.

So, Jessa's mom decided to give medication a shot on a trial basis and put Jessa on the medication the doctor was recommending. The results were incredible. She began to notice a big change in Jessa very quickly. She was able to focus for longer periods of time, her grades began to improve, and she was less disruptive in class and at home.

Jessa's mom found that a combination of therapy and medication was what her daughter needed in order to keep her symptoms in check and begin to get better. Jessa's mom no longer worries about her daughter taking medication, and actually acknowledges that it is making a tremendous positive impact in her daughter's overall wellbeing.

Today, Jessa is a well-adjusted little girl, who can still be a handful at times, but is nearly a different person than just a year or so ago.

CHAPTER THREE

ADHD Setbacks & Maintaining Your Progress

In this chapter, you will learn:

- ADHD Setbacks

- Maintaining Your Progress

ADHD Setbacks

Slip ups or setbacks in your progress can happen to anyone at anytime. The fact is, most people will experience stronger symptoms of their ADHD from time to time. The goal is not to let those small setbacks get the best of you. Remember, every step back is a new opportunity to grow from.

I always like to give the example of learning how to ride a bike when you were young. At first you would fall and be unsteady, but as long as you got up and continued to try, eventually you would learn how to keep your balance and avoid the same pitfalls that seemed so daunting at first. Developing new emotional and social skills is a big process. You'll constantly be challenged with things that feel unnatural and foreign but it's how you learn to adapt to those challenges and overcome obstacles that will define you as a person going forward.

There are several reasons for a setback to occur. Emotional and physical stresses are two of the most prevalent reasons for people's ADHD symptoms to flare up. If you get stressed, you need to take the tools you learn in therapy and apply them to your life. Remember, there's no obstacle that can't be overcome. Keeping a positive outlook will serve you well in the future.

As you begin getting deeper into your treatment and have begun to progress through all of the goals you've set for yourself, realize that the issues you're facing today are just a tiny blip on the radar screen. Most of these things won't matter or even be remembered come a day, week, or month from now. If you begin to notice a growing amount of setbacks on a more frequent basis, follow the steps below to prevent a major flare-up of your symptoms.

Identify the early warning signs and symptoms. A few examples are if you begin losing focus quicker and more often, getting more forgetful on a daily basis, getting anxious more often, or feeling like your entire world is starting to spin out of control.

Considering working more on your emotional and social skills. Go over all the skills you've begun developing in therapy (e.g. social skills training, learning to think before acting or speaking). Are you still using these new skills as often as you could be? If not, try implementing them more into your daily life. Try and work them into your routine, so that it becomes second nature to you.

Also, keep a positive attitude. Having a good outlook will help you in the long run. The ability to find the best in a bad situation will allow you to persevere through even the darkest of days. Remember, setbacks aren't failures.

Having a support system is another vital element. It's incredibly important you have someone you can sit down with and have a meaningful conversation. This doesn't mean more therapy where you're pouring out your heart. It means just finding that person you can vent to, and discuss all your goals with, along with what's happening in your life at that moment. Problems will often seem much bigger in your head. Once you start hearing your issues spoken out loud it can really help to give you some much-needed perspective.

Aiden's Story

Aiden suffers from a severe case of ADHD. He was diagnosed at an early age because he presented many symptoms, and he was struggling with them a great deal. His parents tried to only use therapy, but it wasn't enough. Once they came to that realization, they quickly acquiesced to their doctor's opinion and put him on medication.

Over the next year, Aiden had a great deal of ups and downs. At first, he responded really well to his new regimen of medication and therapy. Soon however, the doctor had to begin adjusting the dosage. A few months later, when that no longer worked, they switched medications. A month later, they switched again, and went to antidepressants.

During this time, Aiden's emotions and state of mind were constantly in flux. At one point he would feel normal and like himself, the next day he would feel like he was spinning wildly out of control. Schoolwork was a daily nightmare and he had trouble relating to other kids his age.

Throughout it all, Aiden always stayed upbeat. Even when he felt at his worst, Aiden would always put on a brave face and try to face the day with a smile. Aiden's parents had drilled into him at an early age that staying positive would help him make the best of any negative situation out of his control. He clung to that idea and it really helped to see him through those dark times when they were still figuring out a treatment that would work consistently.

Eventually, the doctors hit upon the right medication and dosage levels and Aiden's symptoms have been greatly reduced. Dealing with ADHD symptoms is still a daily part of his life, but he knows even when it gets bad that he has the strength and mindset to get through it.

Maintaining Your Progress

It's very important to keep in mind all the positive progress you've made during your time spent in treatment. When you reach a goal, it's good to give yourself a little pat on the back and really try to embrace those moments. Giving yourself positive reinforcement is a way to keep yourself encouraged to keep on practicing and applying all the new skills you've developed. Maintaining your positive gains during treatment requires you to continue working on your social skills, stick to your treatment and medication regimen, and constantly educate yourself on new strategies to overcome any obstacles your ADHD tries to put in your way.

I've always been a big fan of keeping a journal and documenting progress. I believe it's a useful tool both creatively and as a means to look back and see all the progress you've achieved over time. I got my sister and nephew into doing this once they were diagnosed, and they've found it gives them motivation on those bad days when things are tough. Having a journal allows them an easy way to go back and see in their own words all the good that has happened, and all the progress they've made.

Julian's Story

Julian wasn't diagnosed until he out of college. He had always felt different from his schoolmates and family, but refused to confront the fact that there might be a problem. Instead, he would make excuses and find reasons to explain his behavior.

His girlfriend once sat him down and told him she thought he might need professional help. Julian shrugged it off, and it wasn't until months later when his girlfriend broke up with him and he snapped at work, which got himself fired, that he actually considered she might be right. Julian looked up his symptoms online and quickly realized he might have ADHD.

Julian got his suspicions confirmed and immediately began treatment. It took some time and a lot of therapy but eventually Julian was able to get his ADHD under control, and for the first time ever, he felt like a regular person. Over the next few years, Julian had the occasional setback, and once tried unsuccessfully to go off his medication. However, once he learned that he needs to vigilant about his wellbeing, he forced himself into a good place and has a daily routine in place that helps keep him at peak form. Julian is now in good relationship and no longer lets his symptoms dictate the course of his life.

Conclusion

Thank you again for purchasing this book. I hope you've taken something from the stories I've shared with you about these inspiring individuals. Each and every one of them were able to get their ADHD under control and create a happier and more fulfilled life for themselves.

Dealing with ADHD isn't an easy process and it will take hard work and the ability to face your issues head on. Don't get discouraged if the first treatment you try isn't a perfect fit. Over the years, I've met many individuals who've gone through multiple therapies and medications before finding a path that worked for them. Remember, you may also have a few setbacks along your journey. Try to go easy on yourself and keep telling yourself that every challenge you face is just a new opportunity to learn and grow from as a person.

The best advice I can give is that in order to succeed, you first need to accept and love the place you're in now and just be excited for the upcoming challenge, whatever that may be. Coming from a place of positivity always works out better than starting out thinking you're in a hole.

I hope you found the ideas and treatments in the book helpful. If you think you or your child may be suffering from ADHD, I stress that you go see a doctor and get a proper diagnosis. You can't fight an enemy if you don't know what the enemy is. The longer you avoid seeing someone professionally, the worse your symptoms may get. Help is out there and waiting for you. All you need is the courage to ask for it.

I wish you all good health!

BONUS #1 – FREE EBOOK

Go to:
http://planetearth.leadpages.co/grantanderson/

BONUS #2 – $20 OFF VOUCHER FOR GOAL-SETTINGCHALLENGE.COM

Offer code: ebook20

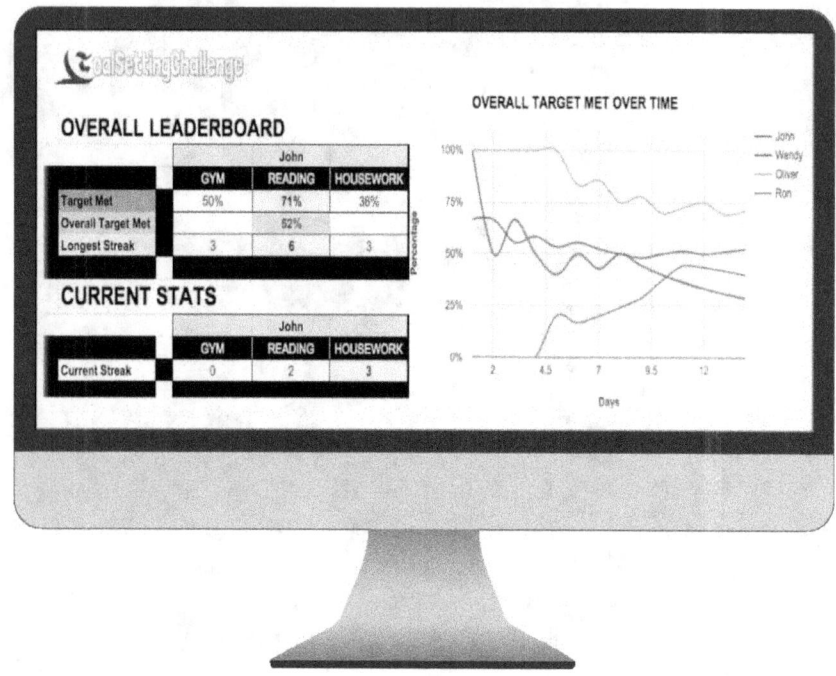

DEPRESSION

STORIES OF THOSE WITH DEPRESSION AND HOW THEY HELPED THEMSELVES

GRANT ANDERSON

SOCIAL ANXIETY

STORIES OF THOSE WITH SOCIAL ANXIETY AND HOW THEY OVERCAME SHYNESS

GRANT ANDERSON

I Need Your Help...

I really want to thank you for reading this book. I sincerely hope that you enjoyed it and that it helped you in some way.

If you received value from this book, then I'd like to ask you for a favor. Would you be kind enough to leave a review for this book on Amazon?

I'm just starting out writing books and it's hard to get noticed being new. Getting more reviews will help me get more exposure.

I really appreciate your help :)

Thank you for your time!

Grant Anderson